Sisters

★ OF ★

SCITUATE LIGHT

Stephen Krensky

★

ILLUSTRATED BY
Stacey Schuett

Dutton Children's Books

Special thanks to David Ball at the Scituate Historical Society,
and Jeremy D'Entremont, noted lighthouse historian (www.lighthouse.cc),
for their invaluable help in recreating the original Scituate lighthouse.

———————————— ★ ————————————

DUTTON CHILDREN'S BOOKS
A division of Penguin Young Readers Group

Published by the Penguin Group
Penguin Group (USA) Inc., 375 Hudson Street, New York, New York 10014, U.S.A.
Penguin Group (Canada), 90 Eglinton Avenue East, Suite 700, Toronto, Ontario, Canada M4P 2Y3 (a division of Pearson Penguin Canada Inc.)
Penguin Books Ltd, 80 Strand, London WC2R 0RL, England • Penguin Ireland, 25 St Stephen's Green, Dublin 2, Ireland (a division of Penguin Books Ltd)
Penguin Group (Australia), 250 Camberwell Road, Camberwell, Victoria 3124, Australia (a division of Pearson Australia Group Pty Ltd) • Penguin Books
India Pvt Ltd, 11 Community Centre, Panchsheel Park, New Delhi - 110 017, India • Penguin Group (NZ), 67 Apollo Drive, Rosedale, North Shore 0632,
New Zealand (a division of Pearson New Zealand Ltd) • Penguin Books (South Africa) (Pty) Ltd, 24 Sturdee Avenue, Rosebank, Johannesburg 2196,
South Africa • Penguin Books Ltd, Registered Offices: 80 Strand, London WC2R 0RL, England

LIBRARY OF CONGRESS CATALOGING-IN-PUBLICATION DATA

Krensky, Stephen.
Sisters of Scituate Light / by Stephen Krensky ;
illustrated by Stacey Schuett.—1st ed.   p. cm.
Summary: In 1814, when their father leaves them in charge of the Scituate lighthouse
outside of Boston, two teenaged sisters devise a clever way to avert an attack by
a British warship patrolling the Massachusetts coast.
ISBN: 978-0-525-47792-1 (alk. paper)
1. Massachusetts—History—War of 1812—Juvenile fiction. [1. Massachusetts—History—War of 1812—Fiction.
2. Lighthouses—Fiction. 3. Sisters—Fiction. 4. Scituate (Mass.)—History—19th century—Fiction.
5. United States—History—War of 1812—Fiction.] I. Schuett, Stacey, ill. II. Title.
PZ7.K883Sis 2008   [Fic]—dc22   2007028297

Published in the United States by Dutton Children's Books,
a division of Penguin Young Readers Group
345 Hudson Street, New York, New York 10014
www.penguin.com/youngreaders

Designed by Abby Kuperstock

Manufactured in China • First Edition
1 3 5 7 9 10 8 6 4 2

For Laura and Julia,
two sisters who also make a good team

S.K.

For Lesly—a steady light always,
in seas calm or rough

S.S.

S*cituate Light* was a welcome sight to sailors at sea. Twenty-five feet high with eight equal sides, it towered over the rocky shoreline south of Boston.

The light was a warning as well. Don't get too close, it reminded the ships sailing by. Dangerous winds and currents are lying in wait.

Rebecca and Abbie Bates knew all about these things. Their father, Simeon, was the lighthouse keeper, and they lived right next door in a house with three rooms and three fireplaces to match.

When they were younger their father had told them stories of ships running aground or sinking in terrible storms. They had marked every word, especially when the wind was howling and the waves tumbled over the rocks.

Running a lighthouse wasn't easy, and all the Bates family helped out. They trimmed the wicks on the lamps, wiped soot off the lanterns, and polished the brass fittings. The chores went on and on, and when they were done, it was time to start over.

After dark, the lighthouse lamps had to be refilled with whale oil several times a night. No matter how hot or cold or nasty the weather got, the light must never go out.

But not only American ships used Scituate Light. It was September of 1814, and the United States was at war with England. The British navy was the greatest in the world, and its ships harried the American coast at will. Only weeks earlier, the British fleet had attacked Washington City, and its soldiers had set fire to the White House.

Later that month, Simeon Bates took most of his family away on a short trip. But he didn't leave the lighthouse deserted. He asked Rebecca and Abbie to stay behind and keep watch.

His daughters kept busy cooking and cleaning. Their most important job, though, was looking out for ships in distress.

But the closest vessel, a British warship, was actually looking for trouble.

Two months before, it had raided Scituate harbor,
taking supplies and burning a few boats.

The townspeople had not dared to protest. Anyone who
interfered would have been killed at once.

Now the warship had returned. The barges had been
lowered and launched toward shore. The beach was empty.
No alarm had been raised.

The British marines smiled grimly. Clearly, they had caught
the Americans napping again.

But Abbie was awake. She had been looking out over the water. Now she ran to find her sister.

"What shall we do?" she cried out to Rebecca. She knew the British were up to no good. "Here are their barges coming again, and they'll burn up our vessels just as they did afore."

There was no time to warn anyone. The girls could flee to safety, but that would leave the town exposed.

"We cannot stand idly by," said Rebecca. "We must do something." But what chance did they have against trained soldiers?

Suddenly, Rebecca had an idea. "You get the old drum up in the garret," she told her sister. "And I'll play my fife."

Abbie looked confused. The drum? She didn't know how to play the drum.

"All you've got to do is call the roll," Rebecca explained.

Abbie didn't see how that would help, but there was no time for questions.

The British boats had almost reached shore when their
officer motioned for silence. The sailors shipped their oars.
Was that music they heard?

The sound of a fife and drum drifted toward them from beyond a grove of trees. The tune was familiar. It was that silly Colonial song "Yankee Doodle."

Confound those Americans! Someone must have seen them. The fife and drum meant soldiers were coming. It could be a regiment or even a battalion.

But there were no American soldiers marching behind the trees—only Rebecca and Abbie playing as loud as possible. Abbie wanted to know what was happening, but Rebecca advised caution.

"We must keep out of sight," she whispered. "If they see you, they'll laugh us to scorn." Rebecca did not add that if the British captured them, who knew what their fate would be?

Finally, they chanced a look. There was a signal flag flying from the warship's mast. Retreat! was the order. The British captain had good ears, and he had heard the music, too.

Abbie was excited and began to speak.

"Don't make a noise," said Rebecca. "You make me laugh, and I can't pucker my mouth."

Now the men in the boats saw their flag as well—and their oars slapped the water. It was one thing to bully a little town. It was another to fight a pitched battle. They turned about so quickly that one marine fell overboard and had to be hauled back in.

Rebecca and Abbie could hardly believe it. The fight was over—and nary a shot had been fired.

They had quite a story to tell when their family returned. The war went on for a few more months, but the British never troubled the town again. The sisters of Scituate Light had seen to that.

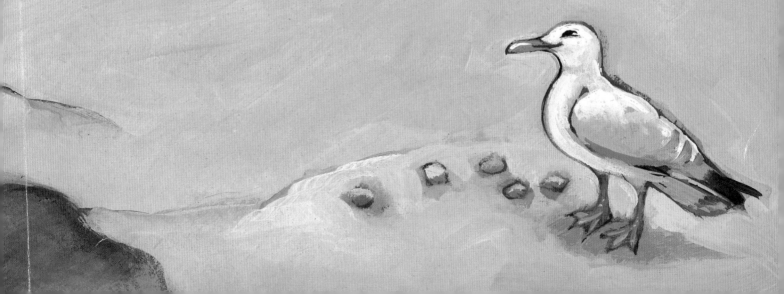

The War of 1812 started for several reasons. There were British ships abducting American sailors at sea and forcing them into their own service. Meanwhile, on the northern and western frontiers, British agents were fostering unrest with Canada.

The war finally ended in 1815. Neither side could claim a real victory, but both were tired of the conflict. Twenty-one-year-old Rebecca and seventeen-year-old Abigail were later hailed as heroes in Scituate for their quick thinking. The dialogue included here is quoted from the girls' own words, taken from magazine interviews they gave many years later. As Rebecca explained, "I was fond of military music and could play four tunes on the fife. 'Yankee Doodle' was my masterpiece."

Luckily for Scituate, it was the right tune at the right time.

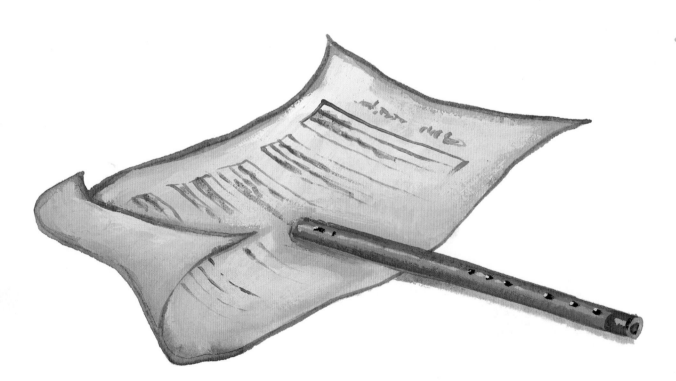

Yankee Doodle

Yan-kee Doo-dle went to town, rid-ing on a po - ny, stuck a feath-er

in his hat and called it mac-a - ro - ni. Yan-kee Doo-dle keep it up!

Yan-kee Doo-dle Dan-dy! Mind the mu-sic and the step and with the girls be han-dy!